SYRIA

CRADLE OF CIVILISATIONS

The author would like to express here his affection for the warm-hearted Syrian people, and his gratitude to the state authorities, who did their best to help him whenever they could.

British Library Cataloguing in Publication Data.
A catalogue record for this book is available from the British Library.

ISBN 0 905743 997

Copyright © 1996 Stacey International
128 Kensington Church Street, London W8 4BH

First published in French in October, 1995
by Vilo, 25 Rue Ginoux 75015 Paris

Set in Sabon by MATS Typographic Services

SYRIA

CRADLE OF CIVILISATIONS

Text & Photographs
ALAIN CHENEVIÈRE

Editor
MARK PETRE

Translators
EMILY READ
MARTHA READ

STACEY
INTERNATIONAL

INTRODUCTION

Syria, in the heart of the Middle East, derives its name from ancient Assyria, the generic classical Greek word describing the stretches of land lying between the Mediterranean and Mesopotamia. After many changes of size and shape throughout the centuries, the present borders were finally set in 1946, the year the country achieved independence. It has an area of 185,180 square kilometres and is bordered to the north by Turkey, to the east by Iraq, to the south by Jordan and Palestine, and to the west by the Mediterranean and Lebanon. It is now called the Arabic Republic of Syria (Al Jumhuriyah al Arabiyah as Suryah in Arabic). It should be noted that the Syrian government demands the restitution of the Golan heights, lost during the Six Day War, and does not recognise France's gift of the Iskenderun (formerly Alexandretta) district to Turkey in 1939.

The towns of the Middle-Euphrates make Syria the cradle of the oldest civilisation of the world, but it is above all the site of the most extraordinary cross-fertilisation of nations and civilisations in the history of humanity. Indeed, more than any other state in the Mediterranean and the Middle East, Syria is the result of a mingling, over millennia, of races and their different cultures, who have left marks on its land and on its soul. The most extreme symbol of this can be seen in the character of Damascus, which sees itself as the capital of the Arab world, the "magical" city which Mohamed himself would not visit, stating that "you can only enter paradise once."

CONTENTS

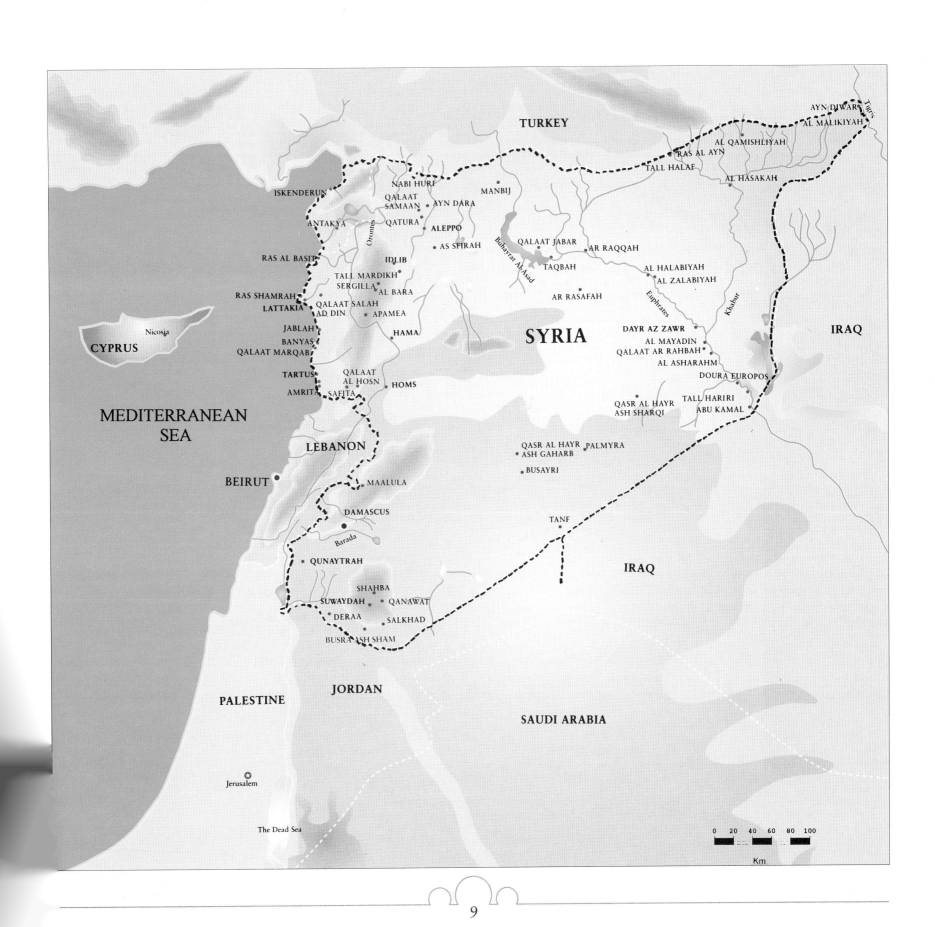

TURKEY

AYN DIWAR
AL MALIKIYAH
AL QAMISHLIYAH
RAS AL AYN
TALL HALAF
AL HASAKAH

NABI HURI
QALAAT SAMAAN   AYN DARA   MANBIJ
ISKENDERUN
QATURA
ANTAKYA   ALEPPO
                 AS SFIRAH   QALAAT JABAR   AR RAQQAH
RAS AL BASIT   TAQBAH   AL HALABIYAH
                 IDLIB   AL ZALABIYAH
TALL MARDIKH
SERGILLA   AL BARA   AR RASAFAH
RAS SHAMRAH   QALAAT SALAH   SYRIA   DAYR AZ ZAWR
LATTAKIA   AD DIN   APAMEA   AL MAYADIN
                         HAMA   QALAAT AR RAHBAH
JABLAH   AL ASHARAHM
BANYAS   DOURA EUROPOS
QALAAT MARQAB
                                                                    QASR AL HAYR   TALL HARIRI
TARTUS   QALAAT   ASH SHARQI   ABU KAMAL
            AL HOSN   HOMS
AMRITA   SAFITA

CYPRUS
Nicosia

MEDITERRANEAN
SEA
                                                    QASR AL HAYR   PALMYRA
                                                    ASH GAHARB
                                                      BUSAYRI

LEBANON

BEIRUT
            MAALULA

        DAMASCUS   TANF

        Barada   IRAQ

    QUNAYTRAH

            SHAHBA
    SUWAYDAH   QANAWAT
        DERAA   SALKHAD

    BUSRA ASH SHAM

IRAQ

PALESTINE   JORDAN

                SAUDI ARABIA

Jerusalem

The Dead Sea

0   20   40   60   80   100

Km

I
A LAND OF CONTRASTS

*G*eographers usually make the distinction between the north, also called the "green delta", irrigated by several rivers (the Orontes, the Euphrates, the Kabir, the Tigris), and the desert south. However, in deference to the physical, climactic and historic individuality of each region, we have chosen to distinguish between five large areas: the region of "Greater Damascus", which extends to the Druze country; the Mediterranean coast and mountains; the furrow of the western plains fron Aleppo to Homs; the fertile crescent, including both the cultivated steppes of the north and Jazirah (Syrian Mesopotamia); and finally the desert.

The mountainous Mediterranean region in the Kabir Valley supports terraced cultivation

THE NATURAL ENVIRONMENT

A young peasant leads his herd of goats down from Jabal Adh al Aziz.

A foreigner, before visiting the country, might well imagine Syria to be a desert country where nothing lasting can grow. Added to this is a ready-made image in the collective imagination which reduces it to a land of the past, full of monuments and museums and nomads wandering on desolate plains. All this is far from the truth. Syria is one of the most lively, dynamic and verdant countries of the Middle East.

A DIVERSE GEOMORPHOLOGY

Syria is formed from an enormous crystalline base dating from the primary era which was flooded several times by the sea and covered in sediment before undergoing an intense volcanic period from the Miocenian Age onwards. The ancient base emerges in the centre of the layer of sediment and basalt, forming the desert in the centre and the east of the country. Earth tremors have created low central folds, in particular the western mountain ranges which reach their highest point in the 2,814 metre high Jabal ash Shaikh (Mount Hermon). These take the form of the high Anti- Lebanon range in the south, and the range of plateaus in the north, lower, but rising gradually as they near Turkey.

The whole mountain zone contains many faults and fertile depressions, the largest of which are the collapsed plain of Al Ghab and the valley of the Orontes. The south is made up of the tabular accumulations of the Hawran and the low volcanic elevations of Jabal ad Druz.

A HIGHLY DIFFERENTIATED CLIMATE

There are three types of climate in Syria: Mediterranean, semi-continental and desert continental. These include many variations according to the type, layout and altitude of the land. The narrow coastal strip and the west face of the mountain range over-hanging it have a Mediterranean climate. There, the four seasons are clearly differentiated, though spring and autumn are much shorter than winter and summer. There is a fairly narrow range of temperature throughout the year (12°C to 26°C) and the rain-fall is relatively abundant (800mm of water per year on average). In winter, snow is common on peaks above 1,200m. The area of the steppes, which is cut off from Mediterranean influence by the coastal ridge of mountains running from north to south, is characterized by low humidity (the average yearly rainfall does not exceed 300mm), and a considerable difference in temperature between summer and winter (from 10°C to 33°C on average). It gets very hot in the summer, and temperatures can reach up to 55°C in Jazirah. The intermediary seasons of spring and autumn are practically non-existent.

The precipitation in the huge Syrian desert is under 100mm per year. The lack of rivers and the scarce rainfall give it a dry continental climate, with large temperature differences between day and night, especially in the winter. The summers there are very hot (40°C on average).

A RELATIVELY POOR FLORA AND FAUNA

Plant-life in Syria is fairly minimal. Until the fifteenth century, forests were abundant and harboured many large animal species; kings and lords would come to hunt them, sometimes from as far away as Baghdad or Cairo. Since then, the uncontrolled clearance of the forest by successive populations together with natural depredation by animals have considerably reduced the wooded areas. A few large forests have survived clinging to the tops of the western mountains. There one finds Mediterranean species: oak, pine, yew, olive, juniper and carob. The steppes are mostly made up of graminaes and bushy, bulbous plants. The desert supports a very sparse vegetation, mostly short grasses and small thorny plants. Several plants are used by the Bedouins for medicinal, cosmetic or culinary purposes.

Animal life there is naturally balanced. Today it is fairly rare to see wild animals in Syria, but wolves, foxes, jackals, gazelles, birds and various rodents still live in the west and the south of the country. Snakes, lizards and scorpions abound in the desert.

Plant-life in the desert is just sufficient to sustain a few animal species; but it flourishes in wet or well-irrigated regions.

*Some families still live in the ruins of
once-thriving ancient Byzantine cities.*

THE PEOPLE

*This engraved
stela dates from
the time of
Emperor Aurelius*

*T**he ethnic make-up of the population of Syria is as complex as
its history. The two basic native races, the Indo-Europeans
and the Semites, have been invaded by continual waves of conquerors and new immigrants since the beginning of time.*

A HETEROGENOUS POPULATION
In simple terms, one could say that originally the west coast of
Syria was populated by Mediterraneans of Indo-European origin,
whereas the rest of the country was occupied by Semitic peoples.
Not only have these two groups intermarried in the course of the

centuries, but other groups have been added to the mixture. Semites (mostly Arabs), Indo-Europeans, such as the Persians or the Armenians, then western and central Europeans. The result is that it is nowadays impossible to attribute a definite origin to any individual. This is all the more true as a new ethnic distribution based on religious differences has been taking place since the Middle Ages. Indeed, for Syrians, belonging to a particular religious creed is of greater importance than any traditional ethnological criteria. Thus 85 per cent of the population are Muslim, 10 per cent Christians, the remaining 5 per cent consisting of diverse small religious minorities such as the Nestorians, the Chaldeans, and the Jews.

Among the Muslims, the most numerous are the Sunni, but

This engraved Hittite stela from the Classical Age (14th century BC) depicts a confrontation between two divine kings.

almost a quarter of the Islamic community is made up of Alawites, Shiites, Ismailites and Druzes. The principle Christian faiths are Greek Orthodox, Greek Catholic, Armenian Catholic, Maronite, Roman Catholic and Protestant.

Thus, Syria's particularly turbulent history is responsible for the heterogeneity of its population and for the geographic distribution of its many ethno-religious minorities. The great link between all Syrians, despite their many differences, is their common language, Arabic, which was brought over in the 7th century by the soldiers of the Prophet, and is now spoken by all Syrians of whatever religion.

A TURBULENT HISTORY

The oldest human remains excavated in Syria, on the banks of the Orontes and the Kabir, are a million years old. The first signs of continuous human settlement have been found to be from the Paleolithic Period (in Al Latamnah) to the Neolithic Period (Al

Muraybat). However, we know relatively little of these primitive cultures, as archaeologists have been most interested in the fabulous "treasure" left in Syria by antiquity.

The chronological primacy of Syria

Recent excavations in Jazirah, in the north-east, cast a completely new light on previous archaeological certainties. For a long time it was believed that Jazirah was an area of transition between the more ancient great civilisations of Persia, Iraqi Mesopotamia, Egypt and Turkish Anatolia, and that therefore it had played only a secondary role in the cultural and political development of the Middle East. But archaeologists have brought to light some very ancient towns which were by turn capitals of empires or kingdoms, and great centres of the caravan trade which for thousands of years linked the ports of the Persian Gulf to those of the Mediterranean basin. The most ancient sites are about 11,000 years old, the most sophisticated over 7,000 years old, which places the various Syrian civilisations amongst the most important in the region. During the next two millennia, the civilisations of Halaf, Sabi, Abyad, Ras Shamrah (Ugarit), Tall Brak and many others shone in all their glory. But above all, we know today that the great agricultural zone enriching the fertile crescent, enabling it to exercise its exceptional cultural influence, first grew up in the Jazirah region, placing Syria at the heart of Middle Eastern civilisation.

From the Semites to the Akkadians

These brilliant civilisations gradually weakened through the ages and could no longer defend their land or their culture. Towards the third millennium, warrior peoples of Semitic origin – the Amorites, then the Canaanites – established themselves along the coasts of Palestine and Syria. Notably they founded the state of Mari on the Euphrates in around 2800 BC. The writings of nomadic merchants boast of the fertility of these regions, and the development of local agricultural techniques soon began to attract the envy of the great Mesopotamian and Egyptian empires.

In Mesopotamia, the powerful King Sargon of Akkad, who had unified all the kingdoms of the south under his rule, undertook the invasion of the lands to the east of the Euphrates, including Syria. He established one of the most formidable empires of antiquity, extending from present-day Iraq to the eastern Mediterranean. He also set in hand a flourishing trade with the other great empire of the region, Egypt.

The rivalry between the Egyptians and the Hittites

Akkad's power diminished from 1700 BC onwards. The western part of the Middle East became the stake in a hidden struggle between the Egyptians and the Hyksos, a race of Asiatic invaders who had established themselves in the north. The Egyptians, led by Kamose of Thebes, stirred up revolts against the Hyksos occupiers in Palestine and pushed them back to their northern bases. Successive pharoahs then sent their armies to the interior of the country towards the Euphrates. Thutmose I probably reached the banks of the river around 1520 BC, but was forced to turn back in the face of the fierce resistance from the native population. Despite several rebellions, the most important of which took place in 1480 BC, Syria remained under Egyptian rule for over a century. Only the small empire of Mitanni, which united several principalities in the Kabir basin in northern Mesopotamia, managed to preserve its independence.

In around 1330 BC, a new force appeared on the Middle Eastern political scene. These were the Hittites, Indo-Europeans from central Turkey who had distinguished themselves three cen-

Winged animals are depicted in this bas-relief from Tall Halaf (9th century BC).

turies earlier by completely destroying Ebla, one of the most renowned Syrian capitals. One of their kings, Suppiluliumas, first seized the Mitanni empire, then embarked on the conquest of northern Syria. The Pharaoh Ramses II came to power and immediately resolved to vanquish the Hittite forces. The confrontation came in 1296 BC at Qadesh (present-day Tall an Nabi Mindu) on the Orontes. This was one of the most bloody and famous battles in antiquity. The outcome was unclear, as both sides claimed victory. The Egyptians were forced back to Palestine, leaving the land to the much-weakened Hittite coalition. The two countries ended up signing a peace treaty in 1284 BC, which gave Palestine to Egypt and Syria to the Hittites.

The Invasion of the "Sea Peoples" and the new Semites

In the course of the 13th century BC, the eastern Mediterranean saw several waves of sea-borne invaders, described by the ancient texts as "Sea Peoples". Historians nowadays agree that these invaders were mostly of Aegean origin, possibly with some Anatolian groups from the west. The Egyptian empire, weakened by internal struggles, could do nothing to loosen these new arrivals' hold on Palestine. In the north, the Hittite state, also beset by terrible rivalries, suffered a violent collapse. One of the main factions, the Philistines, occupied the coastal plain of Canaan, which they called Philistia (origin of the later name of Palestine), whereas other, Semitic, peoples settled in the east. The Edomites settled down to the south of the eastern bank of the Jordan, the Moabites to the east of the Dead Sea, the Ammonites on the edges of the Arabic desert and the Aramaeans on the western banks of the Euphrates. These last then created several kingdoms, the most important of which had Damascus as its capital.

This Roman mosaic (2nd-3rd centuries AD) was discovered at Apamea.

The Hebrew Supremacy

After their exodus from Egypt, the Hebrews had settled in the hills of Transjordania at about the same time as the "Sea Peoples" were invading Palestine. It was only two centuries later that they entered into direct conflict with the Philistines. At first they suffered heavy setbacks. Their troops were destroyed at the battle of Ebenezer in 1050 BC. But King David defeated the Philistines near Jerusalem and decided to conquer the land east of Jordan. He attacked the Aramaean kingdom of Damascus, inflicting heavy losses. By the end of his reign, the cities of Edom, Moab and Ammon (the future Amman) had passed into Hebrew rule. The Philistine kingdoms and all the tribes to the east as far as the Euphrates paid an annual tribute to Israel. With the succession of his son, Solomon, Israel's golden age began.

He equipped his country with a remarkable political and economic infrastructure and established trade relations with Africa, Asia Minor and Arabia. At his death, the Hebrew territory was divided into the kingdom of Judea in the south and that of Israel in the north. The Aramaean State of Damascus, which had rebuilt its forces, quickly challenged the authority of the kings of Israel. One, King Omri, decided to ally with the Phoenicians and attack them. But the other principalities of southern Syria, in particular the city of Moab, took advantage of the situation to rebel and assisted Damascus. Despite his efforts, King Omri could not suppress the Aramaean kingdom. An armed peace established itself between the two protagonists.

The Assyrian, Babylonian and Persian Invasions

In 722 BC, the armies of the Assyrian King Sharrukin (Sargon II) invaded Syria and devastated Israel, driving out most of the population to make way for Syrian and Babylonian settlers. He granted a limited autonomy to the kingdom of Judea, which had agreed to collaborate with him. In turn, the Assyrian forces gave way in the face of Nebuchadnezzar, an ambitious Babylonian king who seized Nineveh, the capital of Assyria, in 612 BC. Thus Syria passed into Babylonian hands. It was then the turn of the kingdom of Judea. Nebuchadnezar destroyed Jerusalem on two occasions and deported the Hebrews to Babylon.

In 539 BC, a new sovereign of Persian origin, Cyrus II, conquered Babylon. He allowed the Hebrews to win back Judea. Under his rule, the Middle East was able to enjoy a relatively peaceful period.

The Greeks and the Romans

In the course of his struggle against the Persian Empire, the illustrious Alexander the Great, king of Macedonia, invaded Syria in 331 BC; when he died, it passed into the hands of one of his generals, Antigonos. Another Macedonian leader, Seleucos the 1st Nikator, became governor of Babylon, where he founded the Seleucid dynasty. In 305 BC he annexed Syria and made Antioch (Antakya) his capital. For 240 years, the Seleucid order ruled the whole region, despite the resistance of the Lagides of Damascus. This period was marked by a thorough Hellenization of arts and customs. In the meantime, a new military and ecomonic force had emerged in the western Mediterranean: Rome. Confrontation was inevitable. In 188 BC, the army of Antiochus III was beaten and the king forced to abandon all his possessions in Asia Minor. From the 1st century BC onwards, Parthian incursions into northern Syria became more and more frequent, posing a threat to the eastern frontiers of the Roman provinces. In 64 BC, the consul Pompey's generals challenged the armies of the Parthian king Mithridates, seized all the great Syrian cities (Aleppo, Hama, Homs, Damascus) and deposed the last Seleucid king Antiochus XIII. Western Syria and Palestine were regrouped at the heart of the Roman province of Syria.

Several Parthian and Mesopotamian kings, with the help of Palestinian and Syrian rebels, tried in vain to invade the province. In 70 AD, Titus destroyed Jerusalem, but maintained good relations with the kingdom of Damascus and the Syrian principalities, which had retained a degree of autonomy. In southern Arabia, the Nabatean kingdom, a large economic power, took advantage of the situation and attempted to take control of the

trade routes between Arabia and the Mediterranean. At the same time another city, Palmyra, was beginning to attract attention in the east. The Romans put a brutal end to the Nabatean ambitions, but as they were about to turn against Palmyra, the Persian Sasanians, who had succeeded the Parthians, invaded northern Syria in the 3rd century. Palmyra sent troops to support the Romans; once friendly with Rome, the city soon became the head of a vast central Syrian empire. But the agressive policies of the ambitious Queen Zenobia eventually tired her powerful protector. In 272, Emperor Aurelius attacked her army, defeated it and razed her city.

The Byzantine Period

When Emperor Constantine converted to Christianity, he founded a capital on the site of ancient Byzantium which he named after himself, thus laying the foundations for the future Byzantine empire. With the death of the emperor Theodosius I in 395, the Roman empire was divided into two halves, the western Empire and the eastern one, which became known as the Byzantine empire. The latter would last for over a thousand years, during which many churches were built in Syria. Now a very important Christian centre, the country was subject to constant attacks from the Persians, who pillaged Aleppo in 540 and Damascus in 614. The Syrians found it hard to accept the complete domination of Byzantium and of its religion. Thus it welcomed most Christian and anti-Byzantine "heresies": Nestorianism, Monophysism, Monothelism.

From the 6th century onwards, the Byzantine empire had to confront another Persian invasion. In 611, the Persian king Khosrow annexed Syria. In took until 622 for the Byzantine army to remove him; he was supported by the Syrian population, who saw him as a liberator from the Byzantine yoke.

The Arrival of the Muslims

Already weakened by many wars, the Byzantines then suffered invasions by the Arabs, warriors from the south. The soldiers of Mohamed were well received by the Syrians, especially the Aramaeans. In 636 the Arabs, helped by a large Syrian contingent, won the battle of Yarmuk. They seized Mesopotamia, Israel and then Egypt. Syria, lying at the crossroad of the great caravan routes and the pilgrim routes to Mecca, naturally became the centre of the new Arabic empire. The governor of Damascus, Muawiya, proclaimed himself fifth Caliph (successor of Mohamed) in 658 and founded the Omayyad dynasty which would last for almost a century. He made Damascus the capital of a huge empire stretching from Spain to India. This was the golden age of Muslim Syria.

In 750, the Abbasids, descendents of Al Abbas (an uncle of Mohamed), overthrew the Omayyads. They made Baghdad their capital. Syria and Palestine suffered a long period of decline, marked by the appearance and disappearance of several local

Mosaics, like these from the 5th and 6th centuries preserved in the caravanserai of Maaret an Numan, adorned the houses of the many surrounding Byzantine cities.

...nasties. Around the year 1000, with the weakening of the ...bbasid Caliphate, Palestine and south-west Syria passed into the ...nds of the Egyptian Fatimids, whereas the north was governed ...y the Hamdanids of Iraq.

The Crusades, the Mamluks and the Ottomans

...1098, Pope Urban II preached the first crusade. After having ...ken Antioch (Antakya), the Crusaders won a series of rapid vic-...ories over the divided Arab principalities. One year later they ...ounded four Christian states, Antioch, Odessa, Tripoli and ...rusalem. These towns, at first ruined by the Crusaders' mas-...cres, enjoyed new prosperity thanks to trade with the west. A ...urkish chief, Nur ad Din (Nureddin), then united all the Syrian ...rritories which had not been conquered by the crusades. He ...efeated their troops in Egypt, and his son Salah ad Din (Saladin) ...ontinued his work. After dethroning the Egyptian Fatamids in ...171, he conquered the Crusaders at Hittin in 1187, taking most ...f their citadels. The western presence remained on the coast as a ...sult of the Third Crusade. Syria enjoyed a new golden age ...nder the Ayyubids, the descendents of Salah ad Din. The ...amluks, ancient Turkish mercenaries who had taken power in ...gypt, succeeded them. Their most famous sultan, Baybars I, ...united Egypt and Syria under his power in 1302.

...The "Mamluk peace" reigned over the whole of the Middle ...ast until the end of the 14th century, when it was threatened by ...series of disastrous events: epidemics, famines, and above all ...e bloody Mongol invasions of Timur Lang (Tamburlaine), an ...zbeki chief who sacked Aleppo and Damascus in 1400. In ...516, Ottoman Turkey was set to dominate the Mediterranean ...nd Middle Eastern world. This enabled Syria to enjoy ...nequalled commercial prosperity.

European intervention

...1830, the Egyptian Ibrahim Pasha, encouraged by the French, ...ok Syria from the Ottomans. The latter had their rights rein-...ated by the British, who did not like to see Egypt with so much ...cal power. But the European intervention brought to the sur-...ce the latent problem of the religious minorities in Syria. The ...hristians, close to the west, tried to take advantage of the situa-...on to impose economic and political dominion. This resulted in ...860 in a violent revolt of all the Muslims in Syria. Almost 5,000 ...hristians were massacred in Damascus alone. The French army ...tervened under the pretext of protecting them. Under French ...le, Syrian society was transformed by the activities of mission-...ies and civil servants, with privileges reserved for a sort of ...hristian aristocracy.

Syria between the two World Wars

...1909, the Young Turks movement took power in Ankara. The ...tivities of this intransigent paramilitary group provoked ...rough its activities the renaissance of strong nationalist feelings throughout the Arab world. Thus during the First World War, Syria became the setting for fierce fighting between the Turks, supported by the Germans, and the Anglo-French troops. The most notable event otherwise was the union of the three sons of the Sharif Husayn ibn Ali of Mecca – Ali, Faisal and Abdallah – on the Anglo-French side, thanks to the activities of Colonel Lawrence (the famous Lawrence of Arabia). In exchange, the allies had promised the Arabs independence. But the promise was not kept because of a secret agreement, known as the Sykes-Picot Agreement, made between France and Britain in 1916. At the end of the war, after the disintegration of the Ottoman empire, a Syrian national congress proclaimed the independence of "Greater Syria" but in vain. In 1920, the Allied supreme council (SDN) entrusted Syria to France and Palestine and Jordan to Britain.

The French created four states, Greater Lebanon, Aleppo, Damascus and the Alawite country, and two seperate districts, the Iskenderun region and the Druze region. A violent anti-French revolt broke out in 1925. It was repressed after a year of fighting and bloodshed. In 1939, for purely political reasons, France returned the region of Iskenderun to Turkey. In 1941, the British army and the Free French attacked the French armies of Syria and Lebanon, which answered to the Vichy government. Lebanon surrendered after a hard battle. After a final joint inter-vention by the French and British to quell a new revolt in 1945, Syria finally gained independence. The last French soldier left Syrian soil the following year.

II

FROM GREATER DAMASCUS TO THE DRUZE COUNTRY

Port Said Avenue is one of the main arteries of the modern city.

*D*amascus is the administrative and cultural capital of Syria. But it consists of more than just the city. It sprawls out into the surrounding regions, draining much of their population off into the suburbs, where all the Middle Eastern ethnic groups co-exist. The term "Greater Damascus" often signifies a geographical entity which encompasses the mountain ranges to the north, mainly inhabited by Christians, and whose influence extends all the way to Hawran and Jabal al Druz in the south, where the Druze live.

COSMOPOLITAN DAMASCUS

Sus *(liquorice water) and* tamarhindi *(Indian date-flavoured water) vendors are one of the attractions of the old town.*

*D*amascus *is the largest city in Syria. Over two million people live in this ancient metropolis that the Arabs call Ash Sham or Dimashq. It is an ancient prehistoric centre that the Sumerians knew as Anshukurraki ("Place of the Horses"). Various excavations, beneath the Omayyad mosque in particular, have unearthed objects which prove that the city was already an important centre for the caravan trade over 5,000 years ago, and that it drew visitors from all directions.*

A TURBULENT EXISTENCE
The city has seen the passage of all the invaders that have crossed the Middle East. Egyptian texts have described a Dimashqa conquered by their troops in about 1500 BC. Around 1000 BC, it fell into Hebrew hands, then into those of the Assyrians in

*Ancient mingles with modern in the urban agglomeration of Damascus,
as seen from Mount Qasyun.*

The impressive size of the Great Mosque of the Omayyads shows that it was originally intended to be the largest sanctuary of the Muslim world.

732 BC, the Babylonians in 600 BC, the Persians in 530 BC, the Macedonians in 331 BC, the Nabateans in 85 BC, and the Romans in 64 BC, who made it their regional capital until the 4th century AD. At this point, the majority of the population of Damascus was Christian. In 661, the city became Muslim. Up until 750, it sheltered the Omayyad Caliphate. When the Abbasids made Bagdad their capital, Damascus fell into relative oblivion. But in 1076, it recovered its past importance when it was occupied by the Seljuk Turks. Under Salah ad Din, it became the capital of a united Egypt and Syria. Then came the Mongols, and then the Mamluks. In 1516, Damascus fell into the hands of the Ottoman Turks. At the heart of their vast empire, it then became a provincial capital of average importance for four centuries. It was only in 1946, with the end of the Second World War, that the ancient city finally became the brilliant capital of the independent Syria.

The Treasure Dome is a small octagonal building on the west side of the inner court of the Great Mosque. Public funds were once kept there.

The western ambulatory is lined with intricately decorated porticos.

ANTIQUITY AND MODERNITY

The old town is the historic heart of Damascus, spreading to the south of the river Barada. It consists of interweaving narrow and twisting streets which house some of the largest suqs of the Middle East. Its inner limits are defined by the remains of the walls which have surrounded it for over 2,000 years. These ramparts have been built, destroyed and rebuilt several times. Those which have survived are Roman and date from the 13th century. The old parts of Damascus contain genuine architectural treasures left behind by the successive occupiers. Palaces, temples, churches, *medressa*s and *hammam*s are everywhere. Among the

The exterior walls (here the south facade), the ceilings and the mirhab *are decorated with gilding and fine mosaics which the faithful have consistently maintained over the course of the centuries.*

most famous are the superb Omayyad Mosque, built in 705 by the sixth Omayyad Caliph, al Walid, who wanted to build the largest mosque in the world. Its construction, in the eastern part of the temple of Jupiter, required a thousand workers who worked for ten years. The three minarets have been successively renovated by the Ayyubids, the Mamluks and the Ottomans. Next to the mosque is the mausoleum of Salah ad Din, surmounted by a reddish dome. The walnut cenotaph dates from the Ayyubid era and the marble tomb was a gift from Emperor

Above: *The Azem palace, with its alternating white limestone and black basalt, is a typical example of Ottoman architecture. Today it contains the Museum of the Arts and Popular Traditions of Syria.*

The mausoleum of Salah ad Din adjoins the north wall of the Great Mosque.

Only a few columns remain of the ancient Roman temple of Jupiter; they mark the entrance of the great covered suq of Al Hamadiyah.

William. The beautiful mosque of Al Walid and the *medressa*s of Al Adiliyah and Al Zahiriyah also deserve a mention. The palace of Azem rises to the south of the mosque. Built in 1749 by Asad Pasha al Azm, the governor of Damascus, this palace has always been considered a haven of peace in the heart of the noisy city. The columns of the 3rd century temple of Jupiter rise at the end of the great Al Hamadiyah suq. It was built on the remains of a very ancient Aramaean temple erected in the 9th century BC in honour of the god Adad.

The Al Hamadiyah suq is the best-known in Damascus. It runs along the walls of the ancient citadel, which was rebuilt several times.

But Damascus is far from being a museum town. It takes its role as a Middle Eastern capital very seriously. Apartment blocks and large avenues are scattered throughout the modern city. Sahat ash Shuhada, the square of the Martyrs, is at the heart of the city. From it radiate the great arteries of Sayd as Jabri, Khaled ibn al Walid, of Ath Thawra and of An Nasr which contain the majority of large hotels, ministries and shops.

In the city's many suqs, stalls sell everything imaginable
to the myriad crush of Damascenes
and strangers

*The superb mosque of As Saydah Zaynab
was built in the southern suburbs with
Shiite funds brought mostly
from Iran.*

THE WORKING CLASS SUBURBS

Damascus is surrounded by a belt of satellite towns. Many of the ethnic (Kurds, Turks, Iraqis, Palestinians) and religious minorities, the Shiites in particular, live there, especially on the lower slopes of the Jabal Kasyun (Mount Kassioun) which are covered in small and modest homes, huddled up next to each other around the many mosques. Relations between these minorities are sometimes stormy, but the authorities are constantly on the alert to avoid conflagration.

South of Damascus lies another Shiite stronghold, the splendid mosque of As Saydah Zaynab, built mainly with Iranian money in honour of Mohamed's grand-daughter. It draws a growing crowd of Shiite pilgrims, many of whom travel from Iran. A real Shiite town has grown up around it, the faithful having purchased most of the local shops. It is now a sensitive zone and foreigners should be wary of giving any signals that could be seen as provocative in the eyes of a people deeply committed to fundamentalism.

*The eastern flanks of the Anti-Lebanon range,
away from the influence of Mediterranean winds,
appear as low arid mountains.*

THE CHRISTIAN MOUNTAINS

This Byzantine icon represents St George slaying the dragon.

*T*he arid mountains to the north of Damascus, the eastern foothills of the Anti-Lebanon, have an average height of no more than 1,000 metres. This region – difficult to get to, hard to cultivate and isolated from the great axes of communication – is inhabited by the greatest concentration of Christians in Syria. These descendants of the earliest Christians zealously continue to celebrate the ancient rites and customs of their forefathers.

BIBLICAL AND MONASTIC LANGUAGES

Scattered around the region are small villages built on the tops of rocky outcrops or nestling in deep valleys. The small fields are arranged in terraces along the slopes, where the labour is often tough. Most of the inhabitants are orthodox Catholics.

*The heights around Maalula shelter several dwelling sites
and rock tombs, some of which date back
to the Neolithic Period.*

The village of Maalula with its facades covered in ochre, blue and mauve-tinted whitewash, is inhabited by a sizeable community of orthodox Christians.

The Convent of Saydnayah, where these two magnificent icons were found, was built on the site where the Virgin appeared to Emperor Justinian

Traditions are so deeply rooted here that, in some villages, very ancient languages are spoken that have not survived anywhere else. Thus Aramaic, a dialect dating from the 1st millennium BC, is spoken in Maalula, Jubbadin and Bakhaa.

There are many monasteries, convents and churches in the region. The two most renowned, which contain the most venerated sanctuaries, are Saydnayah and Maalula.

There are several prestigious monuments in Saydnayah, including the patriarchal convent containing the "Icon of the Marvels", one of the four painted by St Luke the Evangelist. For pilgrims, this convent is second only to Jerusalem amongst Christian sanctuaries of the Middle East.

The convents of St Sergius (Dayr Mar Sarkis) and of St Thecla (Dayr Mar Taqla) at Maalula attract many worshippers every year. The site of Maalula, whose name means "entrance" in Syriac is also famous for the ancient funeral grottos in the surrounding hills and ravines, some of which go back to the Neolithic era.

*The entrance of the the main church, built near the chapel where
the holy icon of the Virgin – painted, it is traditionally
believed, by St Luke – is piously preserved.*

In the peaceful secrecy of a valley dominated by the Krak des Chevaliers lies Dayr Mar Jerjos, the convent of St George.

The convent was built in the 6th century by Justinian and restored in the 19th century. It has always been inhabited by Greek Orthodox monks.

*Low basalt walls separate the plots of land in the characteristic land-
scape of the Druze country.*

THE DRUZE COUNTRY

A young married woman of the Suwaydah region wears her traditional jewellery.

*A*bout a hundred kilometres south of Damascus is the vast and fertile basalt plain of the Hawran which stretches as far as Jordan. Its eastern edges border with the Jabal al Arab and the Jabal ad Druz, two important formations of plateaus and low volcanic mountains which culminate in the 1,765m high Jabal al Drazi. The rocks lend the landscape and the houses a sombre and austere aspect, which is reflected in the character of the inhabitants who have always wanted to remain separate from the rest of Syria.

THE DRUZE PEOPLE
Hawran and Jabal ad Druz, officially called Jabal al Arab, are inhabited by the Druze, a people with very marked characteristics. They belong to a Muslim sect descended from the Shiites and which originated in Lebanon.

Energetic and canny merchants, ferocious warriors and incomparable fighters, the Druze have had a turbulent history. Their fierce spirit of independence has made them naturally opposed to all forms of power. They have in particular continually fought against the Maronite Christians, whom they have massacred several times. Some left Lebanon to settle in Syria around the middle of the 19th century, fleeing French troops who took the side of the Maronites. The region was full of ancient remains, mostly Nabatean and Roman, and they settled among these, using the black basalt stones of the monuments to build their houses. In many families, one or more of the men work in Damascus or abroad and only see their families once a year. Those who remain in the country raise herds of sheep and cows and grow fruit trees and cereals.

To the west and the north,
the rounded hills at the edge of the Jabal ad Druz
overlook the vast fertile plain of Hawran.

*The inhabitants, fiercely attached to their traditions, practise
a particular form of Shiism based on a series of highly
secretive rites.*

The rich town houses were adorned with sumptuous mosaics which are preserved in the local museum and in that of Suwaydah.

SHAHBA AND QANAWAT

This region, inhabited since prehistoric times but set apart from the main axes of communication, only emerged from obscurity during Roman rule. Like most of the surrounding cities, Shahba had its heyday in 244, when the emperor Philip, who was of Arab origin, took control of the Roman empire. The splendour of the small city, called Philippopolis, lasted into the 4th century. Apart from the splendid mosaics (many of these are preserved in the museum of As Suwaydah), the city contains a Roman road, a large altar, a *nymphaeum*, and a small theatre which is almost intact.

Most of the monuments in Shahba were built in the 3rd century,
in honour of the Arab Emperor Philip and his father Martinus.

The best preserved temple of the Qanawat Seraglio, a group of 2nd century Roman sanctuaries, was subsequently used as a Christian basilica, as indicated by the presence of crosses.

The large cisterns of the ancient city are buried among the
foundations of the modern town.

Qanawat was part of the Decapolis, a league of city-states created by the Romans to counterbalance the other regional powers. Once flourishing thanks to its trade with the nomadic centres to the south and the west, Qanawat has now become a sleepy township containing many Roman remains. The most interesting is the Seraglio which grouped several temples in a site considered sacred since time immemorial. The best-preserved building, which dates from the 2nd century AD was made into a basilica two centuries later.

The theatre of Bosra is the best preserved of the Roman World.
It is used for several important annual festivals.

The Seljuk hammam, since restored, was built in the 12th century, east of the mosque of Omar.

BUSRA ASH SHAM (BOSRA)

Mentioned in Egyptian texts as early as 1,300 BC, then by the Romans who named it Nova Trojana Bostra in 106 AD, Bosra is renowned throughout the world for its Roman theatre, the best preserved in the world, which can hold 15,000 spectators. But Bosra is also the Druze mountain town that has experienced the most invasions and occupations. Its appearance bears witness to this. The present town is built in the middle of a pile of buildings and colonnades in various architectural styles: Nabatean, Roman, Byzantine, Arab. Amongst the modern houses, one can also see the ramparts of the citadel, which was much fought over until the 13th century by Muslim soldiers and Crusaders, monumental gates, baths, the Mosque of Omar – one of the three most ancient of the Islamic world according to tradition (most likely untrue) – a cathedral built in the 6th century and a monastery famous for being the site of Mohamed's meeting with the Nestorian monk Bahira, who revealed to him his destiny.

At the main crossroads of ancient Bosra,
the cardo *(the main thoroughfare)*
crosses the road to the Omar mosque
(whose minaret is visible in the background)
near the Corinthian columns of a nymphaeum.

THE MEDITERRANEAN COAST AND MOUNTAINS

The snow-capped mountains of Lebanon, to the north-east, dominate the villages of the Al Buqaya plain

*T*he Syrian coast is only 180 km long. It is however the most densely populated region of Syria, with 86 inhabitants per square kilometre. The coastal plain, backing onto the impressive foothills of the Jabal Lubnan (the Lebanese mountains) to the south, is confined by the dark mass of the Jabal as Amanos to the north. It is bordered all along its eastern side by the rounded heights of the Jabal al Ansariyah, with steep slopes descending to the sea. This volcanic mountain range, formed by violent oreological movements, reaches 1,562m at Al Slinfah. It is covered in a relatively thick forest, especially on its steeper eastern slopes.

A COAST WITH AN ECONOMIC ROLE

The small fishing port of Tartus is protected from winter storms by the perimeter of its stone jetties.

Nowadays, the Syrian coast is the country's most important economic region. It has three major resources. Since antiquity, it has been the natural commercial "lock" between the Mediterranean and the East. It also boasts a rich and intensive agriculture. Finally, since the 1980s, it has become an important area of the oil industry, with pipelines emerging at Lattakia, Banyas (site of the largest refinery in the country) and Tartus.

THE FERTILE COASTAL PLAIN
The series of long coastal beaches constitute what is commonly known as the "Syrian Côte d'Azur". Yet there is no possible comparison with its French equivalent. In fact, the sea is often rough, constant winds blow in from the Mediterranean, and the sand is unfortunately littered with rubbish. Only two beaches, both near Lattakia, are attractive: Shatt as Azraq, where an impressive tourist complex has been built, and especially Ras al Basit, with its black basalt sand and the magnificent natural surroundings of the Jabal as Aqra (the Roman Mount Cassius). Fishing, despite government attempts to develop it, is not profitable and only just

The beach of black volcanic sand of Ras al Basit,
with the mountains of Jabal al Aqra as backdrop,
is considered to be one of the most beautiful in Syria.

supports the small coastal towns devoted to maritime activities.

The narrow coastal plain, which expands to the north, is, on the other hand, extremely fertile thanks to abundant volcanic deposits. The area is farmed intensively as market gardens growing cereals, citrus fruits, fruit trees and tobacco. Olive trees and vines are grown on the higher reaches of the mountain slopes.

*The mountains, especially on their western slopes which receive the
benefits of the Mediterranean climate, are covered in plantations and
abundant flora.*

The peaceful existence of one of the many small fishing villages north of Lattakia is sheltered by a bay.

WESTERN LATTAKIA

The Mediterranean part of Syria is geared towards a trade economy, thanks to the two cities of Tartus and Lattakia. Most of the trade between the Mediterranean and the Middle Eastern worlds goes through the large port of Lattakia (Al Lahiqiyah in Arabic). These places have been inhabited for thousands of years. The modern city is built on the remains of the Ancient Greek town of Laodicea, the port for the prestigious Apamea. Laodicea itself was on the site of Ramitha, a very wealthy ancient Phoenician city. The latter, along with the cities of Apamea, Seleucia and Antioch (Antiakya), formed an extremely powerful tetrapolis which was on an equal footing with Rome until the 2nd century. Long disputed by the Arabs and the Byzantines, Lattakia played an important role during the Crusades, harbouring many Frankish ships. It was then occupied by various powers, including the Egyptians in 1287, and was destroyed several times by earthquakes.

Today, ancient Laodicia is now a modern city with a firmly western culture and economy. It has become one of the most important ports in the eastern Mediterranean.

The present-day city, culturally westernised, has preserved little of its past. It was only from the 1950s onwards that it enjoyed any rapid economic expansion. Its port's international trade places Lattakia at the economic heart of Mediterranean Syria. It is also the site of modern oil and cement-works and of one of the natural outlets of the large pipelines from the east.

The ruins at Ugarit show the square pattern of the paved roads. One can also see the traces of a complex system of water pipes and of the ancient entrance gate to the town.

RAS SHAMRAH (UGARIT)

A few kilometres north of Lattakia, hidden among the green fields, are the ruins of one of the most marvellous cities of ancient times, Ugarit, (Ras Shamrah in Arabic). From 1929 onwards clay tablets were discovered there, which show the oldest alphabet in the world. The engravings were made in Ugaritic, a Canaanite dialect similar to Arabic and Hebrew, during the 14th century BC. Afterwards the alphabet was adapted by the Greeks then by the Romans and is thus the origin of all present Latin languages. Inhabited ever since the Chalcolithic era, Ugarit became an important city from the beginning of the 3rd millennium BC. From the 16th to the 8th century BC, it was one of the richest city-states of the eastern Mediterranean. It was at that time a renowned commercial port, with the advantage that within its walls was a very famous temple of Baal, drawing millions of pilgrims from all directions. Little remains of the sumptuous buildings of the past. But walking among the ruins, one can recognise the foundations of the huge royal palace, the temples to Baal and Dagon, the library of the Great Priest, and the layout of several roads, with their remarkable system of water pipes.

*The main square of the c
town of Tartus is surround
by several mediaev
buildings, mostly dati
from the time of t
Crusade*

MEDIAEVAL TARTUS

Tartus is as traditional and Arab as Lattakia is modern and westernised. Syria's second port, the town seems to fall asleep in winter at the foot of the mountains of Lebanon. The ancient Tortosa of the Crusades and the small island of Arwad which faces it have had a rich and turbulent history, to which their walls bear witness. The Fortress of the Templars and the cathedral of Our Lady are worth a detour. The old town is full of partly collapsed ramparts, vaulted passages, narrow and winding alleys, strong stone walls, stairways and interior courtyards, all dating from the Middle Ages. But the history of Tartus began much earlier. Inhabited since the Neolithic period, it has had several names. The first recorded was the Ancient Greek name of Antarodos.

In winter, the island of Arwad, off Tartus, seems to slumber, watched over by the dark silhouettes of its Frankish fortifications. Yet fishing remains a daily activity.

The walls, with their layers of construction from different eras, bear eloquent witness to the antiquity of the city.

In those days it was a sort of early trading post for the island of Arados (later called Arwad) which had depended on Mediterranean trade since the Phoenician times, when it was a rich city-state of the eastern Mediterranean. In 346, Emperor Constantine renamed the future Tartus Constantina, and made it the main Syrian port. Like Lattakia, it experienced a turbulent history. Conquered, destroyed and rebuilt several times, it became one of the Crusaders' main strongholds in 1102. It resisted the assaults of Salah ad Din in 1188, finally to fall into the hands of the Mamluks at the end of the 13th century. The last Frankish garrison in Syria held out on the fortified island of Arwad right up until 1302. One can still see the two large forts that protected its approaches.

To the south of Tartus rise the mysterious funerary towers of Amrit.
The site has been permanently occupied
since the Phoenician era at least.

AMRIT

Eight kilometres south of Tartus, two tombs adorned with stone lions, called Maghzal and dating from the 5th -6th centuries, mark from afar the site of Amrit, ancient Marathos. We do not have much information on this ancient Phoenician colony, which was captured by Alexander the Great's Macedonians in 333 BC, and then by the Romans. During Roman rule, the town had a brush with the island of Arados. The Romans preferred the bastion out at sea and Amrit quickly lost its commercial importance. The Museum of Tartus contains several funerary objects, including superb sarcophagi found in the still relatively unexplored ruins.

In the interior of the mountain ranges,
many orchards struggle to exist
in a world of white stones.

THE HISTORIC MOUNTAINS

Once through the main gate of the Krak des Chevaliers, a paved ramp leads, after several bends, to the entrance of the inner enclosure.

When the Crusaders took hold of Jabal al Ansariyyah, their first concern was to build fortresses at the summit of the rocky outcrops in order to survey both the Mediterranean and the eastern plains. Throughout the Crusades, these strongholds were bitterly fought over by the Christians and the Muslims. There are many remains. Some castles have lasted well. The three most famous are called Qalaat al Hosn, Qalaat Marqab and Qalaat Salah ad Din.

QALAAT AL HOSN (KRAK DES CHEVALIERS)

Qalaat al Hosn, or the Krak des Chevaliers (*krak* is Kurdish for castle) is the best preserved fortress of the Jabal al Ansariyyah. 750 metres above sea level, it dominates the valley of the Al Kabir river and the plain of Al Buqaya. It was built on the foundations of a fort called the "Akrades Keep" which itself was erected on the ruins of an ancient fortress built several centuries BC, in the fault that separates Jabal al Ansariyyah and the Jabal Lubnan. This gap was a strategic point of the utmost importance, since whoever controlled it controlled all the military and commercial routes in this part of Syria.

Between 1099 and 1110, the Akrades Keep fell into the hands of the Crusaders. From 1141 onwards, the castle was enlarged by the Knights of the Hospital. It housed a garrison of two to three thousand men. It resisted several attacks, but Sultan Baybars forced the last Christians to surrender in 1271, after a long siege. The victor added towers to the fortifications, which lends the fort its special appearance, with Frankish and Muslim styles co-existing. From the top of the ramparts, one can see the *burj* of Safita, or Castel Blanc, a massive tower which, in its present state, dates back to the 13th century. Built by the Crusaders as a staging post between the Krak and the sea, it was damaged by earthquakes and each time rebuilt by the Templars. It was taken by the Mamluk Sultan Baybars shortly after he took over the Krak.

The castle, built on the top of Mount Khalil, majestically overlooks the Kabir valley.

The architecture of the Krak offers an astonishing mixture of Arab and Frankish styles as is shown in the tower of the Daughter of the King (on the top of which there is now a restaurant) and the mosque-chapel.

The township of Safita is renowned for the Castel Blanc, an ancient Crusader tower, now transformed into a fortified church.

Not a single plot of land is left uncultivated. The fields follow the lie of the land, giving the landscape a rounded appearance.

The basalt walls of the Al Marqab fortress form a dark sihouette at the top of a rocky outcrop. It allowed the supervision of the narrow coastal plain and the eastern valleys.

QALAAT MARQAB

The Marqab fort is situated near Banyas on a mountainous spur towering above the Mediterranean coast. It was built in the 11th century by the Arabs on the side of an extinct volcano. The Crusaders conquered it in 1117 and enlarged it. They made it into the largest of the Frankish strongholds, excellently fortified on all sides. It seemed so impregnable that Salah ad Din, who had just won the victory of Hattin against the King of Jerulalem, came up to the walls and did not dare attack it. The castle resisted several onslaughts, but was finally forced to capitulate before the attacks of the Qalawn Mamluks.

Built at the intersection of two small valleys, the castle of Salah ad Din was practically impregnable, especially after the Crusaders dug a trench about thirty metres deep on its northern flank, leaving only a rocky needle to support the draw-bridge.

QALAAT SALAH AD DIN

In the heart of the mountains east of the plain of Lattakia, the Salah ad Din castle, commonly known by the Arabs as Qalaat as Sahyun (Castle of Saone), rises up on a rocky outcrop at the junction of two ravines. The site was occupied from the Phoenician era onwards and several strong-holds were built in succession on one another's foundations. In 975, a huge Arab fortress was erected which was then conquered by the Byzantines. It was then restored several times before being captured by Crusaders in the 12th century. Salah ad Din then managed to take it in 1188 after a long siege. In 1272, it passed into the hands of Sultan Baybars, like many of the forts in the Mediterranean mountains. The most remarkable aspect of the castle is the work the Crusaders put into protecting its northern flank. They dug tens of metres into the rock, leaving only a needle of rock 28 metres high to support the draw-bridge.

IV

THE HISTORIC HEART

*T*he three cities of Homs, Hama and Aleppo, built in the fertile furrow of the Orontes plain, and the western rivers that hug the long depression of Al Ghab, represent the historic heart of the country. Placed as they were from earliest times at the intersection of caravan routes linking the East with the Mediterranean, they experienced an special history which affected that of the whole country. Despite the particular character of each, their structures are all those of the traditional Arab town: a hill in the centre with a citadel on the top, the old town around it, with its mosques and suqs, then the modern residential areas, and finally the often unattractive belt of factories and large commercial and transport companies.

THE ORONTES RIVALS

Left: *At the foot of the mediaeval fortress of Qalaat al Mudiq is an Ottoman caravanserai of the 17th century, now a museum containing an extraordinary collection of Graeco-Roman mosaics.*

The Ibn al Walid mosque, built in the 20th century, houses the tomb of the general of the same name who brought Islam to Syria in the 7th century.

The two cities lie on the banks of the river Orontes (Al Asi in arabic, that is the "rebellious river", referring to the unpredictable floods of this strong current of water originating in the mountains of Lebanon). Up until the middle of the 20th century, they vied with each other for the title of the cultural capital of the Orontes. Hama, with its historic monuments, finally won and Homs got its revenge by becoming an important industrial centre for petrochemicals and refinery.

HOMS, AN INTELLECTUAL CENTRE

Homs (Hims in arabic) with a population of over 600,000, is the third most important city in Syria. Its ancient name is Emesa, not far from the small township of Tall an Nabi Mindu (Qadesh in Arabic), where the Hittites and the Egyptians confronted each other in 1296 BC. The population have always been hard workers and fiercely independent. They ferociously resisted foreign invasions. Their struggle against the Romans is legendary, but their city was annexed to the Roman province of Syria under the emperor Diocletian in the second century. During the following century, having developed into an important economic centre, it became the capital of Phoenicia. Under the Byzantine emperor, it received an episcopal seat and maintained its position until 1260, when the Mongols invaded. After a long period of decline, it regained some of its former glory in the 19th century, particularly when it fell into Egyptian hands. Homs is now a modern and industrial city. Historical monuments are rare. Only the Ayyubid suqs, the palace of Az Zahrawi and the Khaled mosque are worth

Hama is famous for its large wooden norias, *water-wheels which have provided the whole region with water since the Middle Ages.*

the detour. However, along with its geographical position, the city's liveliness makes it worthy of its past.

THE GARDEN CITY OF HAMA

Hama is a very beautiful city. Scattered with parks and flower beds, watered by the Orontes and several canals, where gigantic *noria*s from the Middle Ages still work, it is the "Garden City" of modern-day Syria. Archaeological digs have shown that Hama, the Aramaean Hamath of the Bible, has been inhabited continually since the Neolithic Period. At the end of the second millennium BC, it became one of the most important caravan centres of the Middle East. It was conquered by the Hittites, then by the Assyrians under Sargon II in 720 BC. The latter deported a large part of the population, mainly the ruling class, depriving the prestigious city of its leaders. Later the Seleucids called it Epiphania after their king Antiochus IV Epiphanes. At the beginning of the Christian era, it was named Amath, before being occupied by the Arabs in 638. It regained the name of Hama during the crusades, when the Franks and the Arabs fought bitterly for its possession. Today, Hama is a conservative city, proud of its past and deeply religious.
The town contains many monuments, most of which date from

the Omayyad and Ottoman eras. There are still around a hundred *noria*s in the Hama region. Sixteen of these huge wooden wheels activated by the waters of the Orontes are still functioning. The most impressive has a diameter of 22 metres. Called Al Muhammadiyah, it was built in the 14th century. It used to carry water to the now destroyed Grand Mosque. The latter, modelled on the Grand Mosque of Damascus and built by the Omayyads, was the greatest monument of Hama. One should also note the Mosque An Nuri, built in the 13th century by Nur ad Din, and the Azem palace, built at the beginning of the 18th century by the Ottoman governor Asad Pasha al Azm. The modern city's prosperity comes from the cultivation of cotton, cereals, fruit, and a textile industry fostered by the breeding of silk worms.

The Grand Colonnade of Apamea runs alongside the cardo for 2.2 kilometres between the Gate of Antioch to the north and the Gate of Emesus to the south.

History summed up

Scenes of everyday life were sculpted onto this door-post belonging to a private residence.

*F*ollowing *the course of the Orontes, one reaches the highly cultivated interior depression of Al Ghab. This ancient marsh, intensively drained, has become one of the richest agricultural regions of Syria. According to tradition, the Egyptian pharoahs used to come here to hunt elephants. A thousand years later, the Carthaginians taught the Syrian soldiers to train elephants for war. Al Ghab and the mountainous folds which border it to the east contain remains from the earliest ages to mediaeval times.*

APAMEA, A JEWEL AMONG THE FIELDS
Daily life in the many small villages of Al Ghab moves with the slow rhythm of the seasons, the sowing and the harvests. The

fortress of Qalaat al Mudiq stands on one of the eastern hills. It was built in the 13th century on the ruins of the Apamea acropolis (Afamia in Arabic). Apamea was founded in the second century BC by Seleucus I. Its commercial importance rapidly increased under the Seleucids up until the 1st century AD. It was an important centre of communication between the East and the Mediterranean. A great road linked it to the port of Laodicia (present-day Lattakia). During its period of splendour, about half a million people lived within its walls. This activity continued throughout the Roman occupation, then went into rapid decline with the fall of Rome in the 6th century. The city then fell into

oblivion. Violent earthquakes completed the destruction of its remaining walls in the 12th century. Today, the superb and majestic ruins rise up in the middle of fields of wheat, barley and sugar beet. The impressive central way, which stretches for two kilometres, is lined by cabled, striated or simple columns from the 2nd century which were re-erected in the 20th century. Alongside the road lie the ruins of a theatre, a temple, a *nymphaeum*, or a 5th century mediaeval cathedral. Isolated in an agricultural region, Apamea has been dead for a long time, but its haughty beauty still seduces whoever – tourist or peasant – takes time to look at it.

To the east and north-east of the Al Ghab plain, a series of high parallel hills runs from north to south. The Jabal az Zawitah rises in the middle of these undulations of mineral appearance, covered in piles of greyish stones. There are few villages. The cultivated patches of land seem to have trouble surviving among the ubiquitous loose stones. Yet about 1,200 years ago, this was one of the richest areas of Syria thanks to the cultivation of olive trees and vines. Over 700 towns, long since abandoned, have already been counted.

The columns were re-erected in the 20th century. They date back to the 2nd century. Some have moulded fluting, which is relatively rare in the architecture of antiquity.

Qalaat as Mudiq is an Arab citadel
from the 13th century which was
built on the ruins of the ancient
acropolis of Apamea. There is now
a small village within its walls.

As Sergilla, whose heyday was in the 5th and 6th century, is one of the best preserved of the hundreds of Byzantine city-states south-west of Aleppo.

By the 6th century, agriculture had already turned the region into an important Byzantine economic centre. The numerous city-states, mostly built as early as the start of the Christian era, shared revenues from olives and grapes. But growing rivalries, ensuing conflicts, immigration and the many earthquakes which afflicted the area all led to the gradual desertion of the rich cities. Abandoned and ruined, one after the other fell into oblivion.

Through the course of the centuries, peasants used stones from the monuments to build their own homes. The cultivation of olives and vines did not survive. However, the mysterious atmosphere of these ghost towns has its own particular charm. The best-preserved are Ar Rabyah, Ash Shinshrak, Al Betrsa, Al Bara with its two extraordinary pyramid tombs, and above all As Sergilla, which still has the walls of its main buildings almost intact.

TALL MARDIKH (EBLA)

All that is left of the ancient city of Ebla, (Tall Mardikh to the Arabs) is a pile of shapeless ruins. Yet it represents one of the high points of Middle Eastern civilisation. Founded during the third millennium BC, trade brought rapid prosperity to this powerful city-state. It was destroyed by Sargon II in around 2300 BC, and then again by his successor Naram Sin. It took it about 1000 years to regain its cultural and economic influence, until it was once again devastated by the Hittites in around 1600 BC. It then fell into an irreversible decline. In the small village of Tall Mardikh, which contains the ruins, it is hard to imagine that Ebla was once a splendid city, as testified by the 15,000 or so tablets found on the site, inscribed in Sumerian, which have added enormously to our historical understanding of the Middle East.

From the citadel, we can see the 12th century south gate of the old city.
Access to this is by a small bridge.

ALEPPO AND ITS SURROUNDINGS

The Christian quarters of Aleppo are full of 18th and 19th century houses with beautiful facades of carved wood.

*A*leppo (Halab in Arabic) is the second largest city in Syria. Over 1,300,000 people live there. Built on the banks of the River Kuwayk, it was the capital of the the ancient kingdom of Yamhad at the beginining of the 2nd millennium BC. It was then subject to several Hittite invasions between 1600 and 1500 BC. In the 2nd century BC, it passed into the hands of the Seleucids, who named it Beroia. The city gradually developed what would remain its identifying characteristic until the present day: a fierce desire to live in freedom thanks to trade.

COMMERCIAL ALEPPO

Thus, despite the many occupations it would suffer – those of the Persians and the Arabs in the 7th century, of the Byzantines in the 10th, the Seljuqs in the 11th, the Mamluks in the 14th and the Ottomans in the 16th – and the earthquakes which destroyed it several times, Aleppo throughout the ages was host to hordes of merchants and bankers from France, Italy, England, Turkey, Armenia, Persia, Egypt and Arabia, who were responsible for its

After the fortified enclosure, one passes through several gates, some of which are armoured and studded, to get into the citadel.

remarkable economic infrastructure.

Today, Aleppo, arranged around its Ayyubid 13th century citadel, has become the commercial capital of Syria, since it is located at the intersection of the main routes linking the country to Turkey and Lebanon.

The old town is the most interesting part of the city. There one finds lively and colourful suqs, caravanserais, notably the Khan al Wazir, *hammam*s, including the splendid Yalbuga an Nasri built in 1491, mosques, in particular the Omayyad mosque and the Altun Bagha, and *medressa*s such as Al Ahmadiyah and Ash Shad Bakht. The two Christian quarters of Al Jdaidah and At Taybah contain splendid 18th and 19th century houses.

But modern-day Aleppo does not lack charm. Surrounded by hills of white and ochre stone, excellent for building, the city is full of beautifully refined architecture, apartment buildings as well as individual houses. The cost of labour and material is lower here than anywhere else in Syria and this facilitates property development. The local economy relies on construction companies and cement works, agroalimentary businesses, soap factories, tanneries and a cotton industry. Aleppo has become the commercial capital of Syria and is on the way to taking over from Damascus as the economic centre of the country.

*The wealth of the inhabitants of Aleppo and the low cost of primary
materials allow the building of sumptuous houses and mosques
in the modern city.*

The narghilah *is the traditional Arab pipe. Smoke passes through a container full of perfumed water before entering a long tube, usually made of sheepskin.*

*Craftsmen prepare their wares in the copper suq,
behind Al Kuwatli avenue.*

The covered suqs of Aleppo are among the most famous in the Middle East. Different trades are divided into different areas under the cool vaults.

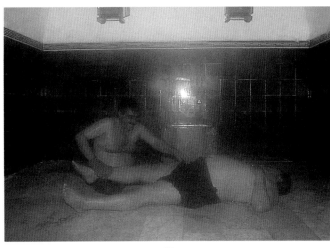

Yalbugha an Nasri,
Aleppo's main Turkish bath,
was built in the 15th century
and restored several times.

At Qatura, the Roman ruins rise up among the houses of a small village. The rock tombs are remarkably well-preserved.

NORTH OF ALEPPO

The steppes which extend from Aleppo to the Turkish border are scattered with very ancient archaeological remains. A goldmine for archaeologists and historians, this relatively unexplored area is nowhere near having revealed all its secrets. Yet the beauty and importance of what has already been excavated gives a good idea of the area's splendour from antiquity to the Byzantine age.

Nabi Huri (Cyrus), Qatura

South of the Turkish border are several Roman and Hittite sites. At Nabi Huri. in an area inhabited mostly by Kurds, lie the remains of Cyrus, a Roman 3rd century city built on the remnants of more ancient cities. Though in a state of ruin, it contains various interesting monuments, including two fairly well-preserved bridges, an amphitheatre and a mausoleum surmounted by a pyramid, a good example of so-called "Romano-Turkish" architecture. The other interesting Roman site is that of the rock tombs at Qatura, a few kilometres from a small and sleepy Syrian village. Above the tombs, sculptures and inscriptions in Greek have been carved into the rock itself.

The Hittite temple of Ayn Dara was built in the 15th century BC in honour of the god of the mountains.

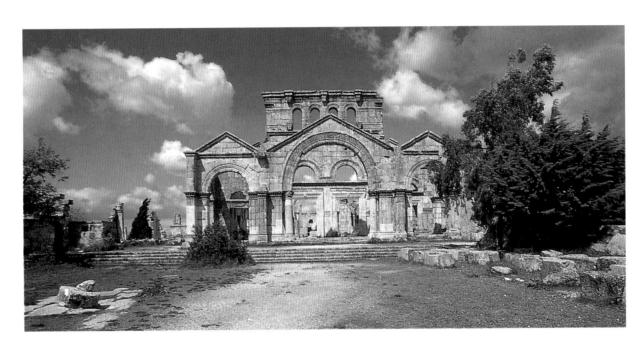

This octagonal basilica, the martyrium, *contains four other basilicas.*

Ayn Dara

The Hittite heritage constitutes one of the archaeological gems of the region. *Tall*s, artificial hills as yet unexcavated and which contain ancient Hittite cities, are everywhere. The most remarkable site, partly uncovered, is that of Ayn Dara. Here, about 1200 years ago, stood a temple dedicated to the god of the mountains. Destroyed and rebuilt several times, the dark basalt buildings contain superb statues, of lions in particular, and several bas-reliefs of winged animals, and friezes.

Qalaat Samaan (Saint Simeon)

Qalaat Samaan is the Arab name for the basilica of St Simeon Stylites. This Christian ascetic led a life that was extraordinary in many respects. Born in Sis in 390, he started life as a shepherd. He then decided, after a divine revelation, to devote himself to a monastic existence. But finding this life not sufficiently redemptive, he became a hermit and went to live in isolation in the mountains. Finally, at the end of his spiritual search, he chose to live at the top of a pillar, whence his name Stylites.

For the next forty years, he changed pillars several times, the last being allegedly 15 metres high. His reputation as a miracle worker drew thousands of pilgrims. Fierce and authoritarian, his neck was attached to the pillar by a chain so that he would not fall while sleeping. He refused to speak to women, not even his own mother. In the end, tired of the veneration of the faithful, he retired to Tall Nashin, where he died in 460. His treatises on asceticism, speeches, letters, hymns and a text preaching the apocalypse have been preserved. When he died, an enormous cruciform church was built around the final pillar, with four basilicas brought together by a fifth in the shape of an octagon. It was completed in 490 and was at the time the largest church in the Christian world. Only the remains can be seen nowadays.

Because of the veneration of pilgrims who over centuries have taken pieces away as souvenirs, all that remains today of the famous column on which sat the Christian ascetic is a large block of stone on a platform.

St Simeon sat in the eastern basilica, the only one with three apses.

V

THE FERTILE CRESCENT

The Syrian part of the Fertile Crescent has maintained its rich agriculture for millennia.

*S*ince the earliest times, the Fertile Crescent of the Middle East has been synonymous with agricultural prosperity and advanced civilisations. Sumerian texts and the Bible even saw it as the site of an earthly paradise. It consists of a series of well-irrigated and highly fertile low plateaus and plains which extend in a vast semi-circle from eastern Iraq to western Jordan, passing through northern Syria. This area, which also contains the course of the Middle-Euphrates, constitutes the north and north-eastern section of the Fertile Crescent, and is generally agreed by archaeologists and historians to be the cradle of the earliest civilisations.

THE NORTHERN STEPPES

The black, originally volcanic, and muddy earth is irrigated by a complex orographical network which feeds lake Asad.

*E*ast of Aleppo as far as the Euphrates are a succession of vast steppes whose fertility depends each year on the abundance and duration of the rains. The inhabitants claim that the strip of land between the Turkish border and the Syrian desert is the richest in the country. The local economy is based on the many agricultural activities of the area, mainly market gardening, sugar beet and pistachios (especially east of Aleppo).

THE TABQAH DAM AND THE CITADEL OF QALAAT JABAR
The northern plains constitute an intermediary zone in economic, ethnic and cultural terms, between Turkey, the Syrian desert and Mesopotamia. Large Kurdish and Turkish minorities have established themselves in the small villages over the centuries, especially in the 19th century. The existence of the great dam at Tabqah has considerably modified the physiognomy of the region and also its economy. Built on the Euphrates from 1963 to 1974, the dam is the pride of the country. It provides a large part of Syria's electrical supply.

Work in the fields is the main activity for the villagers, whose life follows the regular rhythm of the seasons.

An enormous lake, Buhayrat al Asad, over 80 km long and 8 km wide, has formed in the central reservoir. Its water irrigates the whole of northern Syria. The dam should have provided the country with energy independence, but the Turks built another, that of Ataturk, further up the river, which has considerably reduced its flow. This thorny problem has been the cause of some of the worst friction between the two countries.

Qalaat Jabar is on a tongue of land joined to the northern bank of Lake Asad. This citadel, built in pre-Islamic times, was occupied by the Byzantines, rebuilt by Nur ad Din in 1168, and altered by the Mamluks in 1335-1336.

THE "HIVE-VILLAGES"

Scattered around a vast stretch of land running from the Turkish border to the edge of the desert are some astonishing hamlets of earthen houses whose peculiar architecture has earned them the name "hive-villages". For centuries, the inhabitants of this part of Syria, mostly semi-nomadic shepherds and goatherds, have lived in these small conical houses grouped around springs. Today they are used as sheep-pens or store rooms. Some however are still inhabited by poorer families. The most beautiful examples of hive villages are in the As Sfirah region. The walls of the inhabited houses are often white-washed and are located at the centre of the hamlet. Built around these, in concentric cirles or lined up on either side of the homes, other earthen "hives" shelter the herds.

*Inhabited houses are recognisable by their
white-washed walls; the others are
reserved for the animals.*

The "hive-villages", built continuously since antiquity around water points, are falling into disuse. Only the poor families of shepherds and goatherds still live there.

The Euphrates is to Syria what the Nile is to Egypt. Its floods, which carry precious silt, have enabled the reclamation of fertile land from the desert for thousands of years.

THE VALLEY OF THE EUPHRATES

*T*he Euphrates (Al Furat in Arabic) is one of the great mythical rivers of history. Its banks have seen hordes of invaders
and conquerors, many of whom, attracted by the flourishing
prosperity of the area, built some of the most prestigious cities of
antiquity and the Middle Ages. The river rises high in the
plateaus of Anatolia, crosses Syria and Iraq, where it forms a
delta with the Tigris (Ad Dijlah in Arabic) before flowing out
into the Persian Gulf, having travelled 2,430 kilometres, 520 of
which are in Syria. Its flow, once torrential and unpredictable,
has now been reduced thanks to huge dams built along its course.

ABBASIDIAN AR RAQQAH
The town of Ar Raqqah was founded in the 4th century BC by
Alexander the Great. The Seleucids called it Nikephorion.

It later became the favourite place of residence in Syria for the Abbasids. The town was rebuilt in 772 by Caliph al Mansur, with a circular plan modelled on Baghdad. It was renamed Ar Rafiqah when it was chosen by Harun ar Rashid as his summer residence and then made regional capital. It was destroyed in 1260 by the Mongols. There are some interesting remnants from the Abbasid era such as the Baghdad gate and important sections of the wall; from the Ayyubid period such as Qasr as Binaat ("palace of the maidens"); and from the Mamluk period, such as the minaret built by Nur ad Din on the ruins of the Abbasid Great Mosque.

ft: *Agricultural techniques
*ich have changed little since
*tiquity often get in the way of
*e economic development of
e region.

*Of the ancient brick walls and
monuments of 8th century
Ar Raqqah, only a few sections of
the wall remain, near the Baghdad
gate and around the Ar Rafiqah
mosque with its typical minaret.*

The northern steppes are one of the most traditional areas of Syria. In every activity, old methods are meticulously perpetuated.

The river's seasonal floods provide fertile silt each year.

The inhabitants of this part of the Middle-Euphrates carefully preserve the cultural character of their region, especially in their clothing.

One can view the Al Halabiyah fortress on the left bank of the
Euphrates from its counterpart, the ruined Al Zalabiyah.
These two citadels were built in the 3rd century
on the orders of Queen Zenobia.

Despite its size, the suspension bridge at Dayr az Zawr can only be used by pedestrians and two-wheeled vehicles.

THE TWIN CITADELS OF AL HALABIYAH AND AL ZALABIYAH
These two strongholds situated on either side of the Euphrates, Al Halabiyah on the right bank and Al Zalabiyah on the left bank, were built in 272 under orders from Zenobia, the queen of Palmyra, shortly before she was defeated by the Romans. After her downfall, the citadels became Roman, then Byzantine outposts against the Parthians and the Sassanids. Emperor Justinian ordered the rebuilding and raising of the outer wall of Al Halabiyah. The remains are well preserved and can be visited to this day. Al Zabiyah on the other hand, abandoned earlier and hardly restored at all, appears as little more than a pile of shapeless ruins.

Dayr az Zawr is a meeting town between the peasants of the Jazirah and the desert Bedouins. They frequen the suqs, or consult a public scribe. Then the children play while their fathers drink tea.

DAYR AZ ZAWR AND ITS SURROUNDINGS

The city of Dayr az Zawr (Deir ez Zor), on the right bank of the
Euphrates, is the largest city in the east of Syria with a population of around 500,000. A pleasant town, it has acted since
antiquity as an invaluable point of contact between northern
Mesopotamia and western Syria. The discovery of rich oil fields
in Jazirah has brought an appreciable surge to the local economy.

Though very ancient – remains from the Neolithic Period have
been found there – Dayr az Zawr has not preserved one single
significant monument of the past. For the foreign visitor, its main
interest lies in the fact that it is the place of lively and colourful
meetings between desert Bedouins and the peasants of Jazirah
who come daily to buy and sell their products in the suqs.

Right: *Doura Europos,*
large Graeco-Roman c
was famous for
religious toleran

The Ar Rahbah citadel,
built in the 13th century,
was ravaged by
battles between the
Mamluks and the
Mongols.

The south of Dayr az Zawr on the other hand, is scattered with
archaeological sites. The two most remarkable are Qalaat ar
Rahbah, a 13th century Arab citadel which was bitterly fought
over by the Mamluks and the Mongols, and Al Asharahm, a
sleepy little township where remains from the Christian era can
be seen, as well as a small mediaeval mosque made of clay bricks.

About fifty kilometres from the Iraqi border is the imposing
fortified town of Doura Europos, from the Arabic *dura* which
means "wall". Its walls overlook the right bank of the river
Euphrates, which flows 80 metres below. It was founded in the
3rd century BC by the Seleucids. It served as front-line defence
against the Parthians in the Hellenic era, but fell into their hands
in 121 BC. The latter kept it until first Palmyra, then Rome in
165, annexed it. From then on and for several centuries, Doura
Europos was to become one of the most important front-line bas-
tions for the Romans in their struggle against successive Persian
dynasties. The town was known for its tradition of great religious
tolerance. It was taken in 256 by the Sassanids and entered into a
period of irreversible decline, and was totally abandoned before
the end of the 6th century.

To visit the impressive ruins of Doura Europos is to discover
several remarkable cultures side by side. The enormous Hellenic
fortifications enclose Roman, Palmyran and Parthian structures.
Remains have been found of sixteen different religions, among
them temples to Mithra, Artemis, Astagatis, the Gads, a syna-
gogue from the 2nd and 3rd centuries (which has been trans-
ferred to the National Museum in Damascus) and a Christian
basilica from the Byzantine era.

TALL HARIRI (MARI)

Today Mari is confined to a small site, burnt by the sun, facing the flank of Tall Hariri, on the right bank of the Euphrates. It was once however the most prestigious ancient city of Syria and one of the most important in Mesopotamia. It was founded around 2800 BC by Semitic peoples on a more ancient, still undiscovered site. Sumerian texts assert that between 2600 and 2340 BC, the city was ruled by the tenth dynasty in the era that followed a flood also mentioned in the Bible. The city was rapidly enriched by the fall-out from the flourishing trade between Mesopotamia, Anatolia and the Mediterranean.

*The town was enclosed by its walls. On the eastern side,
for a few dozen metres, the walls drop straight down
to the Euphrates.*

This was one of the rich private homes of Mari.

It then underwent a series of setbacks following many military expeditions by the people of Ebla, as well as Akkadians, Sumerians, Amorites and Babylonians. In the 19th century BC, it once again enjoyed a period of splendour which reached its peak under the reign of Yahdoon Lim and, especially, Zimri Lim. Mari was at that time at the head of a veritable local mini-empire. But this prosperity came to a brutal end in 1758 BC when the Babylonian King Hammurabi destroyed the great city of Mari, which was then abandoned. On the present site one can see several houses, roads, five temples, the remains of a *ziggurat* (a Mesopotamian pyramidal tower) and in particular the foundations of two palaces, including that of Zimri Lim which measured 200 by 120 metres.

The sun sets at the confluence of the Khabur and the Euphrates,
not far from Al Mayadin.

SYRIAN MESOPOTAMIA

A woman of Turkish origin makes bread in a village of the Al Qamishliyah region.

A series of fertile plains between the Euphrates and the Tigris to the north-east of Syria, makes up the Jazirah – literally "island" (of greenery) – in the middle of the desert. This is Syrian Mesopotamia, historically and culturally linked to its Iraqi equivalent. This region, whose agricultural role can be traced to the dawn of humanity, has without doubt remained the most traditional of the whole country. But the recent discovery of very important oil deposits has upset the balance of this ancient society.

THE COUNTRY'S GREEN LUNG
Jezirah has the benefit of vast underground lakes and a complex irrigation network built by man throughout the ages. It is watered by three large rivers, the Tigris, the Euphrates and its tributary the Kabir, as well as by the important orographic network which is linked to them. These waterways are subject to a climate of snow and rain which brings about short and fairly brutal floods during the rainy season, between December and

Recent archaeological discoveries have proved that agriculture, the main activity of the present day population, began in this part of the world about 10,000 years ago.

A peasant from the region of Al Hasakah cooks hard wheat cakes in an earthen oven.

February, and longer and more powerful floods when the snow melts between April and May.

Here also is the most fertile land in Syria. The inhabitants, living in the heart of pretty little hamlets, often say that their land is the "country's granary". It was here after all that, according to recent archaeological discoveries, primitive man settled for the first time and invented agriculture, gradually abandoning his hunter-gatherer existence to farn the land. Work in the fields has remained the main activity, subject to the regular cycle of the seasons. Market gardening, fruit trees, cotton and tobacco are the main products. In the 1980s, the local economy expanded rapidly following the discovery of oil and gas deposits, a continuance of the enormous oil fields of Iraq. Over a hundred are being tapped today. The reserves seem to be very large and the Syrian government is planning to speed up the opening of wells. Actual production satisfies domestic needs and the rest is exported. But the arrival of foreign companies, their technicians and many vehicles, the appearance of roads and new industries linked to oil and its derivatives, and the massive influx of money, are in imminent danger of clashing with the old traditions.

Traditional Kurdish villages can be recognised by their distinctive architecture of walls made of large stones.

A traditional life lies at the heart of the many Kurdish communities in Syria, south of the Turkish border.

THE KURDISH AND TURKISH REGIONS

The only towns in the Jazirah are Al Hasakah and Al Qamishliyah. Because of the proximity of Turkey and Iraq, a large part of the population consists of immigrants of Kurdish and Turkish origin who have settled there through the ages. A flood of new immigrants arrived from the 1970s onwards, after the Turkish and Iraqi governments began a merciless campaign against the Kurdish separatists. But the Syrian government succeeded in keeping matters under control and external conflicts have not spilled over into their territory. The sight of the small villages just south of the Turkish border comes as a surprise to the visitor. The clothes, food, domestic architecture, signposts and customs are more reminiscent of Turkey or northern Iraq than Syria.

Pastoral scene, with, as backdrop, the arid heights of the Bibek Dagl in Turkey.

A large population in the north of Jazirah is of Turkish origin. They have imported their customs and their agricultural techniques.

The women, as in most eastern countries, do most of the work.

VI
THE DESERT

*T*he desert alone covers over half of Syrian territory. It is
called the Baduyat ash Sham, the bleakest and most inhos-
pitable region of the country. There the Bedouin nomads, descendents of the first inhabitants of Syria, follow their herds of sheep.
To the north, a large strip of land, a little more watered by the
rain and better irrigated by a system of canals, marks an
intermediary zone between the Fertile Crescent and the desert
proper. Sedentary and semi-nomadic populations live off crops
and herds there.

THE SCORCHED WORLD OF THE BEDOUINS

The desert appears as an enormous monotonous stretch of pebbles scorched by the sun. It continues into Jordan and Iraq where sand takes over from stones, a precursor of the vast Saudi desert. The region is dry and what little rainfall there is is unpredictable and often violent. Then the small streams, normally dried up, swell briefly but violently. A few large oases are dotted around the north of the desert, but their frequency dwindles to the south.

The Badiyat ash Sham is a huge monotonous stretch of ochre stones.

THE BEDOUINS

The desert is the domain of the *Bedu*, the Bedouins, who wander in search of pasture and water holes for their herds. They move over tribal territory along recognised routes, known and mapped

for centuries. To encroach upon neighbouring territory is a serious fault which, in the past, would spark off bloody tribal wars. Today, though aggression is slight, respect for territorial rights is one of the fundamental laws of Bedouin life. According to tradition, the Bedouins are the first "true Arabs", descended from Abraham via two mythical ancestors, Qahtan and Adnan. According to the founding father of the tribe, the Bedouins are divided into the Arabs of the north, sons of Adnan, and Arabs of the south, sons of Qahtan.

The flora and fauna is limited to sparse thorny thickets, and a few species of animals, like this large monitor lizard.

AN UNCHANGING DAILY EXISTENCE

Bedouin life is ordered by the unchanging rhythm of the seasons. In spring, the desert turns green again after the rains. This is the favourite season for the nomads, when they hold their family festivals and weddings. In summer, they have to leave the open desert for the oases; the clans and tribes regroup and sign new agreements. This is the season of the great tribal festivities. When the cooler autumn months arrive, the animals need less water, so the Bedouins once more make their way deep into the desert. Winter nights are often very cold. Once established in their camps, they hunt and breed their animals. Then spring returns and with it a new year begins which will unfold in exactly the same way as those that preceded it.

In the desert, the villages, inhabited by semi-nomads, are simple groupings of low flat-roofed houses.

Springs are rare. Sometimes, during the summer drought, herds are forced to queue for hours before it is their turn to drink.

The Khiyan are the traditional tents of the Bedouins. They often call them bayt as shaar, *"houses of hair".*

The master of the home is the only one entitled to serve his male guests the very strong coffee, flavoured with cardamom.

AN EGALITARIAN SOCIETY

In the hostile desert environment, the individual cannot survive alone. He must therefore be integrated into a highly structured grouping of men. This is the role of the tribe which centres around a strict patriarchal system and draws together all the heads of family descended from the same eponymous ancestor. Bedouin society is based on perfect egalitarianism. Individual property is reduced to a minimum, and the community ensures collective protection for each of its members. The result is a very strong sense of tribal belonging, called *asiliyah*. Executuve power is in the hands of a *sayd* elected by a council of chiefs. Often the term *sayd* is replaced by *shaykh* (Sheikh), meaning "ancient". The basic components are the patriarchal extended families. These units are brought together in clans or tribal sub-factions which unite, according to an established formula, "all the sons of uncles to the fifth generation". These clans are united in the bosom of a tribal sub-division, which itself emerges from an ancient political/military entity. Finally these sub-divisions are grouped in one tribe.

ORAL CULTURE AND TRADITION

Bedouin life is necessarily tough and relatively simple. Their culture on the other hand is far from being simplistic. It is closely linked with a tradition that is lived out from day to day and is the central pillar of family and tribe, and which governs everything. Thus it defines the clothing of the men and women, which has been unchanged for centuries; the food, based around three basic elements: bread, meat and milk, from which is made butter and yoghurt; the structure of the *khiyan*, the famous Bedouin "hair houses". These long tents, whose shape has not changed for centuries, are made out of strips of plaited goat hair. Inside, a curtain separates the men's quarters from the women's quarters. Arms, saddles and pack-saddles are arranged on the men's side. Covers, rugs, goatskins, and the food reserves are heaped in the women's quarters. Two hearths are usually dug in front of the tent. One is for the coffee which only the men are allowed to offer male guests. The other is used by the women to cook. The great flowering of Bedouin oral culture lies in poetry, recitations and music. Though the children do not go to school, or only very irregularly, they are nourished with ancient legends and long monotonous chants in the evening, beneath the tents. The warrior exploits of their ancestors, amorous romances of the past, conflicts between heroes and evil genies are at the heart of the collective memory of the Bedouins.

Beneath the tent, the tea ceremony is complex. Coffee is only drunk,
accompanied by sweet-meats, after it has been offered three times.

A woman of the Suwayr clan in the central desert
nurses her baby .

*Elderly women, released from outdoor work, sew covers and hangings,
reproducing the ancestral motifs of the tribe.*

A Bedouin woman from the Fidan tribe cooks a barley cake on the outdoor fire reserved for women.

Every Thursday, the market of Dayr al Hafr brings together many Bedouins come to sell their sheep and goats.

The Shammar tribe, among whose clans this young married
woman lives, range from the Euphrates to Iraq.
They are one of the largest Arab tribes.

The Ar Rasafah basilica is dedicated to St Serge who was martyred here in around 205. For a time the immense fortified town was called Sergiopolis.

DESERT FORTRESSES

This site, only partly cleared, shelters several religious and secular buildings.

The northern part of the desert was once much greener than it is today. Ancient texts describe it as being covered in thick forest. Without going that far, we do know that the region was scattered with fields and gardens belonging to the great royal families from the 5th to the 10th century. It contains several strongholds and fortified castles from the Byzantine age and the beginning of Islam. Most were abandoned before the year 1000, but their impressive remains survive proudly among the pebbly wastes.

AR RUSAFAH

The dead city of Ar Rusafah lies about 30 kilometres south of the main road between Aleppo and Dayr az Zawr. Mentioned already in Assyrian and Biblical texts under the name of Rezeph, this very ancient city enjoyed a period of great prosperity under the Romans, which reached its peak during the Byzantine rule. In 205, St Serge was martyred there under Emperor Diocletian. A century later, when Christianity became the state religion, he became patron saint of the city, which took the name Sergiopolis.

Right: *The desert is fu of ruined fortresses an palaces. Most dat from the Omayyi and Abbasid era.*

The powerful city of Ar Rasafah was abandoned after the Abbasid armies destroyed it in 743.

The town drew many pilgrims during the centuries that followed. In 616, the Persians under King Chosroes II invaded it. This was the beginning of a long series of disasters for the town. It was conquered in the 7th century by Omayyid Caliph Hisham, then by the Abbasids, and then Sultan Baybars, who deported a large proportion of its population to Hama in the 13th century. The huge wall which protected the town, built by the Byzantine Emperor Anastasius, was almost intact. It forms a 500 by 300 metre rectangle. Inside, apart from the beautiful broad alleyways, one can admire the churches, a basilica, shops and six huge underground cisterns.

QASR AL HAYR ASH SHARQI AND QASR AL HAYR ASH GHARBI
One of these "twin" castles is situated to the west of Palmyra, the
other to the east, as their Arab names indicate. They are reminiscent of the castles of the Jordanian desert but are much larger.
They were built in the 7th century by Caliph Hisham. Large gardens and fields surrounded them. They were important strategic
points on the caravan routes towards Mesopotamia, but were
also used as resting places for the Omayyid and Abbasid kings,
especially Harun ar Rashid, who made them his hunting lodges.
The western castle is badly damaged; but the eastern one, partly
restored, has retained much of its splendour.

Like its western counterpart, Qasr al Hayr al Gharbi, the Castle of the East, was surrounded by huge gardens and plantations in the heart of a region which was in those days heavily wooded.

Qasr al Hayr ash Sharqi is a magnificent example of Omayyid architecture. The famous Abbasid Caliph Harun ar Rashid made it his hunting lodge in the 8th century.

The castle is at the end of an ancient road built through the middle of the desert by the Romans as early as the 1st century.

This votive bas-relief decorates the entrance to the temple of Baal.

PROUD AND SPLENDID PALMYRA

The imposing sanctuary, dedicated to the Palmyrian triad, Baal, Yarhibol and Aglibol, is built on a large, almost square, esplanade measuring about 225 metres square.

*T*he name Palmyra (Tadmoor to the Arabs) has drawn so many visitors over the centuries that this prestigious metropolis has come to symbolise Syria. Nestling beside an oasis of palm and date-trees – hence its Semitic name of Tadmoor, "city of dates" – it is mentioned on Assyrian tablets in around 2000 BC as a caravan stop on the Silk Route that linked China and Europe, via the Middle East. The Romans baptised it Palmyra, "city of palms".

THE MARCH TO GLORY
Palmyra drew its prosperity from taxes imposed on merchants using its roads. Its power grew in proportion to the decline of the power of the Nabatean capital of Perra, which controlled the commercial routes to the south.

The large funerary towers which rise at the entrance to the Valley of the Dead could accomodate several sarcophagi on each floor.

Thanks to the diplomacy and self-effacement of its sovereigns, Tadmor managed to preserve its independence even under the reign of the Seleucids, and to form an economic empire. Its political autonomy came to an abrupt end in the 2nd century BC when Roman legions advanced towards the east and confronted the Persians. Tadmor then became a sort of buffer-state between the two powers. Despite a few hitches, relations with Rome were good from the start. The Emperor Hadrian declared it a free city, and Caracalla gave it the title of Roman colony, giving the inhabitants of Palmyra equal rights with the Romans. The city then enjoyed a period of exceptional prosperity. Caravans from China, India, Persia, the Persian Gulf, Arabia, Turkey and Europe stayed within its walls. It reached its zenith in the 3rd century under the reign of the wise Odenathus II, a brilliant military chief who had saved emperor Valerian from the Persians. Relations between Rome and the man who had saved their leader could not have been better. Emperor Gallianus even entrusted him with the command of the Roman army in Syria, then, after several victories, named him *dux* and *imperator*.

ZENOBIA'S CHALLENGE TO ROME

Then, under circumstances that are still unclear, Odenathus II was assassinated in 266 at Emesa (Homs). His second wife, the beautiful and intriguing Zenobia, who claimed to be descended from Cleopatra, took power in the name of her young son Vaballathus, who was still a minor. Gallianus was opposed to the queen who had no hesitation in taking up arms against her powerful ally. But she was also a crafty politician, and when in 269, Emperor Claudius was facing the invasions of the Goths, she decided to help him by sending troops to support other Roman legions fighting in Egypt and Asia Minor. She was rewarded by Aurelian, who had succeeded Claudius, and who agreed to recognise the royal title of Vaballathus. But this did not satisfy Zenobia's ambition. She expanded her empire, increased the power of the army and despite the leniency and repeated warnings of Rome, proclaimed the independence of the Palmyran empire under her son in 271. War with Rome was inevitable. In 271, Aurelian's legions defeated Zenobia's troops at Antioch and Emesa, then besieged Palmyra. The obstinate queen managed to escape in the night and fled towards Persia. She was captured by the Roman cavalry on the banks of the Euphrates and Palmyra surrendered. Zenobia was taken to Rome and took part in the Emperor's triumph, attached to his carriage by gold chains. In 273, the proud city revolted once again, forcing Emperor Aurelian to raze it.

FROM OBLIVION TO REDISCOVERY

Palmyra never regained its splendour. The caravans took alternative routes. It was taken from the Byzantines by the troops of Khaled ibn al Walid in 634, then destroyed in 745 by Marwan II, the last Omayyid Caliph, after another revolt. In 1089, a huge earthquake ruined it once and for all. Ancient Palmyra entered into oblivion for many centuries.

It was rediscovered in the 17th century by English merchants. Europeans developed a passion for this beautiful romantic city and its tragic fate. Since then, tourists' interest in Palmyra has remained constant.

The ruins, partially rebuilt, are superb. They cover almost fifty hectares. There are many monuments, palaces, columns and tombs. The most famous are the temples of Baal, of Baalshmin and of Nebo, the *hypogeum* of the Three Brothers, the great 1.1 kilometre-long colonnade, the *tetrapylum*, Diocletian's baths, the theatre, the agora, the senate, the banqueting hall, the funerary towers and the southern *hypogea*. There is a superb view of the city from the small 17th century Arab castle of Qalaat ibn Maan.

The tetrapylum *is a majestic set of four groups of four columns. It has been much restored; only the dark granite column is of the period. In the background rises the massive silhouette of the 17th century Arab castle of Ibn Maan.*

The agora *covered about 6000 square metres. To the left is the great banqueting hall.*

The monumental triple arch marks the western entrance to the city. It was built at the end of the 2nd century.

The series of porticos on this road, which ends on the cardo, *leads to the camp built by Diocletian after his victory.*

The Grand Colonnade looks magical at every moment of every day of the year. Its 1.1 kilometres linked the funerary temple and the temple of Baal. Half way up the column, one can see cornices which held statues of sovereigns and important citizens.

ENVOIE

For a part of two days I wound under the base of the snow-crowned Djibel el Sheik, and then entered upon a vast and desolate plain rarely pierced at intervals by some sort of withered stem. The earth in its length and its breadth, and all the deep universe of the sky, was steeped in light and heat. On I rode through the fire, but long before evening came there were straining eyes that saw, and joyful voices that announced, the sight – of Shaum Shereef – the 'Holy', the 'Blessed' Damascus.

But that which at last I reached with my longing eyes was not a speck in the horizon, gradually expanding to a group of roofs and walls, but a long low line of blackest green, that ran right across in the distance from east to west. And this, as I approached, grew deeper – grew wavy in its outline; soon forest-trees shot up before my eyes, and robed their broad shoulders so freshly, that all the throngs of olives, as they rose into view, looked sad in their proper dimness. There were even now no houses to see, but minarets peered out from the midst of shade into the glowing sky, and kindling touched the sun. There seemed to be here no mere city, but rather a province, wide and rich, that bounded the torrid waste.

This 'Holy' Damascus, this 'earthly paradise' of the Prophet, so fair to the eyes, that he dared not trust himself to tarry in her blissful shades – she is a city of hidden palaces, of copses, and gardens, and fountains, and bubbling streams. The juice of her life is the gushing and ice-cold torrent that tumbles from the snowy sides of Anti-Lebanon. Close along the river's edge, through seven sweet miles of rustling boughs and deepest shade, the city spreads out her whole length. As a man falls flat, face forward on the brook, that he may drink, and drink again; so Damascus, thirsting for ever, lies down with her lips to the stream, and clings to its rushing waters.

Even where your best affections are concerned and you – wise preachers abstain and turn aside when they come near the mysteries of the happy state, and we (wise preachers, too), we will hush our voices, and never reveal to finite beings the joys of the 'Earthly Paradise'.

from *Eothen*
A.W. Kinglake
1844

Original idea and graphic design
© Bower
Layout, execution and cartography
Plein Format
Marseille

First published
October 1995by Vilo
English edition published
July 1996
© Stacey International